MAGPIE MORNINGS

poems by

LORA LIEGEL

Finishing Line Press
Georgetown, Kentucky

MAGPIE MORNINGS

For Tegan

Copyright © 2023 by LORA LIEGEL
ISBN 979-8-88838-137-3 First Edition
All rights reserved under International and Pan-American Copyright Conventions. No part of this book may be reproduced in any manner whatsoever without written permission from the publisher, except in the case of brief quotations embodied in critical articles and reviews.

Publisher: Leah Huete de Maines
Editor: Christen Kincaid
Cover Art and Design: Christina Parkinson
Author Photo: Michelle Metzler

Order online: www.finishinglinepress.com
also available on amazon.com

Author inquiries and mail orders:
Finishing Line Press
PO Box 1626
Georgetown, Kentucky 40324
USA

Table of Contents

A Blessing for the New Year 1
Waiting 2
Sun Song 3
Green 4
Beginning 5
The Healer 6
These Hands 7
Home 8
You, Me—The in Between 9
Paper Snow 10
Letters 11
In The End 12
Alchemy of the Unfinished 13
Mess 14
Small Wonders 15
August 16
The Sentinel 17
Myrtle Beach, SC 18
Returning 19
Samara 20
River's Edge 21
River of Darkness 22
Reflections 23
While Walking in the Forest 24
The House 25
Stuck 26
Trillium 27
The Trail 28
Little Lake 29
Kindred 30
Two 32
Heartwood 33
Solstice 34

A BLESSING FOR THE NEW YEAR

The new year is not
a promise nor a guarantee.
The new year does not forget
nor forgive for us—

but the new year does bring hope.

Hope in the stillness
of freshly fallen
snow. Hope
in the budding branches
preparing to rejoice
in the sweetness of spring.

Does the new year appear
when we say hello to the rising
sun? Does the new year bow
when we say goodnight
to the shining
blue stars?

The new year arrives
when we dare to take notice.
Dare to falter
fail and begin again
each time with renewed spirit.

May we hear the knock
of the invitation. May we
open the door. May we feel
amazed by our own audacity to look
out and see every color
we've ever dared to imagine.

May we be blessed
by the new year
its light shining
its candle burning.

WAITING

Rain falls
fast and heavy
onto the pavement below.

Water permeates the slivers of space
where silt is born from stone.

Anticipation leads to ink on a page
running a river of thoughts.

I close my eyes
imagine the idea of our beginning
and finally say hello
to night's repose.

In morning light
you will have arrived
belonging to no one
but yourself

and I'll always remember
while I was waiting for you
I began
to find myself.

SUN SONG

From Nashville to Asheville
sing to me child
and I promise you
I'll play and dance
with a heart that's wild
for all your days to come.

GREEN

I once went
to the Blue Ridge Mountains
but it was their green
that cut me open.

Above and below,
tenderness—
fronds and palms opening,
instinctively reaching to the heavens.

It was the sun pierced canopy
that I could not turn away from,
the hidden layers,
hurriedly unfolding.

I laid my hand on the universe
and felt the pulse of life.

I once went
to the Blue Ridge Mountains,
on the brink of becoming a mother,
and later returned
to say goodbye to my own.

Rumi says, "To be like the leaves
and let the dead leaves drop."

And then, what comes next?

We are the spring buds, reborn,
emerging
into the world
a child,
green, new, whole.

BEGINNING

Shame shatters
at my feet.
I face front, forward.

Looking at the place between
here and there. The shards
of glass no longer sting.

Curled toes wrap around
a thousand tiny grains
of sunlit sand.

Reflections of me and you
merge into one. The mirrors
I thought I saw

were only the remnants
of lines drawn by time.
I see them in the corners

of my eyes
in the carved cracks
upon my hands.

THE HEALER

I don't know
which birds make her sing
or even
if the wind whispers her name.

I do know
there is a sacred place
where four walls, fade and fall
where the window is always left open.

She sets the table
with an invitation,
pure and simple.

Give her your truths
and she'll offer remedy in return.

She shows me
that the path to healing
is in the light
of a million scattered stars

messy and brilliant
strewn across the sky.

When she puts her hand on her heart
I want to set myself
free.

THESE HANDS

These hands have carried silent secrets
for far too long.

They've poured out of me unknowingly
without grace, without favor
crying for attention.

Attention I could not give
until I paused enough
to simply
listen.

But these hands, these hands are learning
to make noise.

These hands are no one else's but mine.

These hands hold choice
and the promise of possibility
and freedom too.

These hands are learning to cradle love
alongside the imperfection.

These hands are learning, slowly, to weep.

HOME

Rest your head
upon my heart
and we'll build a home
that's pure and true.

Looking out the window
I see the orange setting sun
dancing between the leaves.

Small hands
climb confidently
moving among blooms and branches.

Deft arms reach up
to where the earth
touches the sky.

Welcoming the newness
of our vision
you shed your skin

while I say goodbye to mine.
Dusky light
beckons your return.

The door opens—
we step inside.

YOU, ME—THE IN BETWEEN

Twilight's blanket
envelops the room.

I feel the weight of your world
pressed against my skin.

The music of your heart
flows through me
filling the forgotten places.
Blood, bones, lungs.

Previous definitions crack and rift
rearranging the landscape of our future.

Where once there was only white,
now I see snow
falling
in shades from charcoal to silver.

Words reclaim their rightful meanings.

This is you,
a daughter.

This is me,
a mother.

PAPER SNOW

Paper snow falls from the sky
light and quiet.

Crumple the edges,
tear the words,

light a fire,
to hear the crackling pages.

Leaves from a tree
tremble and shake.

Peel off the bark
layer upon endless layer.

Meet me in the middle
where the story unfolds,

feel the unbound margins
imperfect and new.

LETTERS

Swallow wings beat inside my chest
feeling the familiar tug of open space.
Sometimes the hardest part
is just beginning—I think

of all the words you have never heard,
the thoughts, you will not feel,

there is so much
loss it bleads into sadness,
it pours across the pages of my heart
pooling, crimson.

Hope comes somewhere
between the first
and last breath—I think

I don't need some faint idea of you
anymore. I need to breathe.
I need to feel the hot exhale of a
breath, of a body who has lived,

who is
still living.

Live your life and I'll live
mine.

I'll remember when the sunflowers were tall,
leaning heavy against the house,
ready to embrace the arms of autumn,
when the air felt cool and crisp,

when we sat
together, side by side,
when we wore the same shade
for a single moment,

blooming burgundy.
Hands held over our brows,
smiling, squinting into the sun.

IN THE END

My mother died today.

She's not passing. Not going. She's dead. Why do we not talk about death, as it actually feels? Now I'm left to untangle myself from my youth.

In the end, she was my mother. I was her daughter. I loved her. And now, I'm left to pick up the pieces.

Today, I was drawn to my childhood escape, a small hill on the outskirts of a small town. Something we both found beauty in were flowers.

I touched the wild iris. Knelt by the camas. Found comfort in a late-blooming trillium. Open space. Tall green grass. Freedom.

And tomorrow, I will see her face for the last time.

ALCHEMY OF THE UNFINISHED

Eyes close to
see. Tiny. Black. Dots.
Circular stars in transition.

Content among
the words, specks of
dust, rest easily. A period is—

a placeholder
for the in between. The
what comes next. The unknown.

Darkness,
when read by
gentle hand and heart,

illuminates the hidden
places, the stories
not yet written.

Finality ceases to exist. Deep
blue stars grieve; and
receive light.

Orbiting galaxies shine.
Mystery meets me
here—

in the space where beginnings
die, and endings
are reborn.

And
why not? Change
the course. Turn the page.

MESS

When I close my eyes, I see the house that I grew up in—my memories, buried among the detritus and filth. I laud the complex beauties cradled within a life. Paintings stacked haphazardly on the ground—a connection to the healing powers of art. Thousands of scribbled notes and newspapers—an attachment to the allure of ink on paper. Framed photographs tucked away in old cardboard boxes—her love for me and my family. I feel the past colliding with the present. I honor this moment of my life. I see an ending in the nearby distance, that I myself get to write.

SMALL WONDERS

Bleeding hearts
forget me nots

a kaleidoscope
of proof and spent seasons.

Swaying poppies set the median on fire
ablaze in orange and crimson.

Time, always moves to its own accord.

Flames are dowsed by seas of indigo.
Lupine—shares her story.

On the hillside
a budding invitation

awaits
from digitalis—

slow down,

look,
touch,
taste.

The honey bee
enters.

So many small wonders
that this world offers.

If these do not feel big
then what more is there?

If the thorn of the blackberry
did not prick,

how would we know
the pulse of our own hearts?

AUGUST

August is the taste of warm blackberries. The sound of grasshopper wings as feet step into dry grass. It's finding a single moment outside myself. Ladybugs with spotted wings. Caterpillars who will one day take flight. It's a sea of falling petals and singing voices. Reminders to stop and listen.

THE SENTINEL

Tall totems
proudly rooted
where roadside ditch
meets forest edge.

A blurred line
where stalk and leaf
lean in.
Where pink petals, open.

The sentinel speaks—
Ring your mantled bells loudly.

Secrets pour out of you
one by one,
humming against grainy pollen,
sticking to sweet nectar.

Keeper of truths,
friend of fox,
show me
your dreams.

I will close my eyes
to see
soft arrows pointed
in the right direction.

MYRTLE BEACH, SC

Along the shoreline,
toes touch wet sand.

I wade into water,
slowly
feeling the crash of waves
beneath the surface.

The sun's warmth on my back
and curve of sky
assure me—
enough.

I bend,
letting tide take away
ashes and bone
falling through my open fingers.

We part
peacefully.

The rippling remnants of what are left behind
sink to the sea floor.

Among rock and stone
who have held
more than a million lifetimes

we each uncover the undiscovered
and begin again.

RETURNING

You return to grief
to sink into it

not run or hide
but let it wash over you
to embrace the pull

of a thousand perennial tides.
You bend your knees
to feel the salty sand underneath

again and again
you resemble
what you once were

but weathered and bare
you're now something new—
smoother, finer, softer.

SAMARA

A curved end
an angled arch
a meager weight
between two fingertips.

A prickly shell—
holding
the potential power
of transformation.

One
small
seed.

Life.

Friendly hands wave
in the branches above.
Leaves who have spent more than one
season flirting with sun and sky.

A faint breeze announces autumn's arrival.
The standing tree buttons up its bark.

Leaf edges curl and yellow.
Wrinkles meet weathered veins.
Only the wise show such dissent—
so boldly.

Samara finally lets go.
She takes flight,

falling

round and round
centered
to the soft earth below.

Buried by a crisp blanket of leaves
Samara waits for spring.

RIVER'S EDGE

In the damp forest
it's easier to imagine
me
as I know to be.

My hands and heart
lead the way.
At the river's edge
I kneel.

This is where I pray,
in the arms of trees.

I dip my hands
into the cool
flowing water.
History has no hold here.

Sand runs through
my open fingers,
pebbles dance
upon weathered whorls.

In my palm
I cradle a single small stone.
Feeling the weight,
I stand in awe.

Imagining what it once was.
Imagining what it will become.

RIVER OF DARKNESS

I've circled the sun
36 times.

Floating among ancient dust
and distant light.

But my life began before,
in familial shades of blue and green.

When the grass was tall,
when my warmth was born from another.

And then,
beyond that too.

I close my eyes
to see.

Into the river of darkness,
back and behind.

I feel the tug
of my ancestors.

We navigate
these waters.

Mixing and melding,
together and sovereign.

In my own two hands
I hold a wet piece of paper.

Simple lines drawn on a map
guiding me home.

REFLECTIONS

Silent flames
Silver and bright
Shine through
The broken light

In the mirror
I see your face
We share a line
It leaves its trace

But my eyes are mine
I hold my ground
Repeating images split
Unfurling sound

In this new house
Reflections of me and you
The windows I dare to dream
Looking through

What bounces back
Is an infinite me
Past and present
What I brave to see

WHILE WALKING IN THE FOREST

While walking in the forest yesterday
I saw a tree who had fallen

to the ground. At first I felt the
sadness which comes from losing a friend.

The bark lay still and heavy, the inside core cracked.
And then, I looked up and around.

I noticed the azure sky, the green shining leaves.
From cracks of space above and below

new light entered.

I inhaled, rejoiced in delight. For where there is
grief, the fullness of joy enters too.

THE HOUSE

There was a window in a house, godforsaken.
I passed through the nearby door,
in and out, every day,
but never really left.

I used to think, *I could smash that window's glass
and let it all fall to the floor.*
Then maybe they would stop.
Maybe someone else

would hear or see.
I had the bat.
Strong and smooth
made of wood.

But it was only a dream.
The house held on tight.
Its walls gobbled up all the light.
I never felt flying splinters

or broken shards.
The only pieces that pierced my skin,
were apparitions,
haunting and uninvited.

Anger had forgotten its own name.

But still, sometimes I feel it calling.
The desire for fire lingers.
In my mind
I light the wood and watch it burn.

STUCK

There is so much noise I cannot think
She will not shut up and he isn't here
I want to run so far but I'm stuck
These walls are thick I'll never know free

She threatens to slit her wrists
Then smiles to answer the door
The madness will not stop
I pick up the mess off the floor

There is nowhere to go
Two faces I always see
The horrors of this house
The stories that cannot be

I carry this weight inside my chest
So heavy I cannot breathe
Chains on my legs and in my lungs
Yet still somehow I believe

I hold onto myself
Three two one
Count the years
Until they're done

Powerless no
Windows no doors
I don't live
Here anymore

I grit my teeth
Stuff it down
No sound
No me

TRILLIUM

Trillium
soft and sweet

purveyor of the past
keeper of secrets

what is it
that your slender petals
do not say?

THE TRAIL

Falling light
Hills are calm
Fire and ash
Wake up the night

LITTLE LAKE

Little lake
love me so.
Waves rippling
to and fro.

Tall trees
hug me tight.
Branches swaying
through the night.

Midnight mountains
speak your truth.
Rocks splitting
let go of youth.

KINDRED

At the time
I did not know
I cut a fir
to watch it grow.

Looked around
upon the ground,
only broken branches,
dusty tinder to be found.

Rain poured sideways
sun did shine,
water and life and light—
roots who would not die.

From that pollard
alchemy old to new,
the earth soon came alive
with tender wakeful shoots.

I looked inside
that big old stump
and to my surprise,
I did find,

that cut down tree—
was a little me.

In the middle
where the circles
were so round so true,
I dug a hole

with my two bare hands
and planted a tiny seed
which sprouted
into a little you.

Upon the wind
bows and buds opined
our bodies grew and grew
and grew until they intertwined.

That big tall tree is no more
but in its place
two new shades of green,
warn wood, an open door.

TWO

You arrived when a season's end
was knocking outside my door.

Two times now around the sun
And winter crystals fall once more.

That word *Mother* tumbles through my mouth,
under icy frozen sheets, a secret river flows.

I don't know the future, but I can see
the light you hold, while standing in the snow.

HEARTWOOD

In the hollow of an old oak tree
hangs a spider's web
a constellation of points and paths.

I don't know how long
it's been there
but in time

I'll gently sweep away
the sticky threads.
Placing my palm upon

the scarred bark
I'll feel safe enough
to look inside.

A window all along
leading straight
to the heartwood.

SOLSTICE

We wake early
to watch the sun
rise.

One season ends,
another enters.

Looking above,
effervescent light
traces shadowed
hills and weightless clouds.

Time is neither
short nor long.

It is humble indigo
becoming
radiant fuchsia—
alchemy in morning sky.

Even in the absence of light,
may we give thanks.
For we know,
the sun always rises.

AUTHOR'S NOTE

In the winter of 2018, I had a vision of a magpie. I had only seen the birds once before while visiting eastern Oregon a decade earlier. Although the experience was from long ago, the vivid memory stayed with me.

The birds had instantly caught my attention. They seemed weightless, effortlessly hopping from one fence post to another. Their calls were inviting yet haunting. When the sun shown on their wings, colors changed from white to black. Night to day. Dark to light. Iridescent greens and blues vanished just as quickly as they appeared.

When the memory returned, I got out my colored pencils and drew the bird from my vision. I sent the small piece of colored paper to my mother. She too had been drawing recently—simple sketches of flowers and a nearby lake.

Shortly thereafter, my mother died.

When I told someone about my magpie vision, she mentioned that the birds mourn their dead. They announce their presence. They gather around the deceased, arch their heads to the heavens, and release high pitched cries.

While I held my newly born daughter in my arms, hope and grief finally became languages which I could understand.

Poems are visions. Poems are dreams. Poems are prayers. Poems are the hidden layers inside ourselves wanting to be written—waiting to meet the light of morning.

www.ingramcontent.com/pod-product-compliance
Lightning Source LLC
Chambersburg PA
CBHW022124090426
42743CB00008B/996